and I pray
God will prov...
mate for you.
let me know when He
answers my prayer!
Thank you for loving
us from the beginning
and please don't ever
stop!

I Love you,

Gary June '98

P.S. I asked
God to show me how to
say goodbye to my friends
and I found this scripture →
Eph. 1:17-20. Know that this
will always be my prayer
for you.

Design by Elizabeth Woll

Published by The C.R. Gibson Company
Made in the U.S.A.
ISBN 0-8378-8071-8
GB648

For My Friend

Photographs by

Kim Anderson

Poetry by Paula Finn

THE C.R. GIBSON COMPANY, NORWALK, CONNECTICUT

I have shared so much with you.
Your listening helps me
hear my thoughts,
your insight helps me
understand my problems,
and your patience helps me
accept my faults.

You know when I need advice,
and you know when I simply
        need you.

Everything I could ever want
        in a friend
I have in you.

As your friend,
I appreciate your strengths;
I accept your weaknesses.

I do not wish to
judge,
control,
or change you.
You are who you are.

*Y*ou're always there
to help, to encourage,
to remind me that I'm
        not alone.
You're never too busy to be
        a friend.

Thank you for sharing
so much of your time,
your understanding ...
and so much of yourself.

Whenever I need to talk,
you listen.
Whenever I need to be quiet,
you understand.
Whenever I need,
you give.

Your support has truly made a
difference in my self-confidence,
my happiness,
and in my life.

You've forgiven my mistakes,
and helped me to forget them.

You've believed in my dreams,
and helped me to find them.

Because of you,
I am richer—
And I will always be grateful.

You're In My Thoughts Today . . .

I'm thinking of you today and I'm
remembering how often
you've come through for me
when I needed you most—
how you've always given
so generously of your time,
and so freely of yourself.

I'm thinking of how easy it is
to be with you,
how funny things seem even funnier,
and ordinary pleasures feel special
because they are shared.

I'm thinking how often
your belief in me
has made the difference
between giving up on my dreams,
and trying even harder to reach them.

I'm realizing how special you are—
and how much richer my life is
because you are in it.

So today, I'm thinking of you—
of all the good things you've done,
all the kind things you've said,
and all the beautiful things you are.

The he more I know you ...
the more glad I am that I do!

*Y*ou and I...
understand,
accept,
enjoy,
support
and care for each other.

You and I...
are what friendship is all about.

As a friend you've taught me
to believe in myself,
to appreciate myself,
to·trust myself,
to accept myself.

From you,
I've learned to be a friend
to myself.

Each day I discover
how important a friend can be...

And how lucky I am
to have one like you.

You know how to be strong
when I am weak,
comforting when I am in pain,
uplifting
when I am discouraged,
giving when I am in need.

You know how to be my friend.

The strength of our friendship
is honesty;
the comfort of our friendship
is acceptance;
the joy of our friendship is caring;
the beauty of our friendship is us.

We have such good times together!

We see the same things as funny
        or absurd,
and our tastes are the same in
    almost everything.

We can talk for hours
about things that are most important
      to us . . .
We can talk for hours about nothing
      at all.

We relate as equals.
Competition does not exist between us;
power is never important,
but respect always is.

I can confide in you,
and trust you with my mistakes
and my regrets.
I can tell you things I've told
     no one else
and I know you will never judge me ...
or tell my secrets.

*T*hanks for being the friend
who's always believed in me,
who's always understood,
who's always accepted me,
who's always cared.

What we have is rare—
Let us protect it,
celebrate it,
cherish it ...

Let us always be friends.

COLOPHON:
Designed by Elizabeth Woll
Edited by Eileen M. D'Andrea
Type set in ITC Garamond Light and Charme